Introduction by W. Terrence Gordon

Printed originally in *Explorations* 6 (1956), the journal that grew out of the interdepartmental seminar in culture and communications led by McLuhan at the University of Toronto, this essay is his first to be marked throughout by the thrusting and questing style of writing that he referred to as his probes. Like Joshua's trumpet, a McLuhan probe is a clarion call; like the *One-Way Song*, cited in the opening lines below, it sabotages the conventions of prose, offering "paragraphs" as short as half a line; like all media, whose operation McLuhan explores here with its help, the probe is a technology or extension. As such, it occupies a privileged place, for its function is to extend consciousness, the essential function of all language and the key to understanding media. As McLuhan sounds one blast after another through the medium of his probes, he offers us that key by evoking the rudimentary semiotics of animal languages, the incantatory power of language before writing, the effect of writing on the dynamics of the spoken word. His probes suggest as much as they show and show what they suggest, inviting us to move with the author to the bold conclusion that "all languages are mass media, so the new media are new languages." —WTG

The Media Fit the Battle of Jericho

I SABOTAGE THE SENTENCE! WITH ME IS THE NAKED WORD.
I SPIKE THE VERB — ALL PARTS OF SPEECH ARE PUSHED OVER ON THEIR BACKS.
I AM THE MASTER OF ALL THAT IS HALF-UTTERED AND IMPERFECTLY HEARD.
RETURN WITH ME WHERE I AM CRYING OUT WITH THE GORILLA AND THE BIRD.

One-Way Song
Wyndham Lewis

The Western world is living through its own past and the pasts of many forgotten cultures.

We think we are watching the rushes of recently shot film as we let the dreaming historical eye of the projector god entertain us.

Print merely permitted a fixed stereoptic vision of the past. Its imagery-flow was much greater than writing or speech permitted. But it was very far from the simultaneity that came with the telegraph, and which now characterizes all phases of our culture.

The telegraph gave us the global snap-shot which knocked out the walls between capitals and cultures, and created 'open diplomacy', or diplomacy without walls.

Olivier's *Richard III* movie gives as a single experience the specialist knowledge of many historians of English art and society. It would take one person many years to assemble the details of the past that are there made available to the six-year-old and the professor alike. The simultaneous convergence of many kinds of specialist knowledge results in knocking out all specialist walls. It knocks out the walls between historical and biological categories equally. The child can enter the past as easily as the trained archaeologist. History is abandoned to the Bridey Murphys.

We can now move into any past on the same terms at least as the cab-driver possesses the present. The upshot of the minute and exact reproduction of a phase of the English past is that it is as vulgarly familiar as the urban features of our own present.

This is not to point a moral.

The same state of affairs resulting from simultaneity of communication appears in our cities. Cities were always a means of achieving some degree of simultaneity of association and awareness among men. What the family and the tribe had done in this respect for a few, the city did for many. Our technology now removes all city walls and pretexts.

The oral and acoustic space of tribal cultures had never met a visual reconstruction of the past. All experience and all past lives were *now*. Pre-literate man knew only simultaneity. The walls between men, and between arts and sciences, were built on the written or visually arrested word.

With the return to simultaneity we enter the tribal and acoustic world once more. Globally.

As primeval man pressed on his acoustic walls and moved forward the visual orientation of experience, he discovered sculpture and painting as sculpture. Sculpture is half-way to architecture and writing.

Sculpture is not the enclosure of space. It is the modelling of space. But to a purely acoustic culture such a means of arresting visually the dynamics of acoustic space must inevitably appear as very astonishing.

Purely acoustic space, the space evoked by the spoken word in a pre-literate world, is equally magical. The complex harmonic structure of the word can never be a sign or reference before writing. It evokes the thing itself in all its particularity. Only after this acoustic magic has been enclosed in the fixed written form can it become a sign.

To capture the dynamics of the phonetic flux or flash in a fixed visual net—that was the achievement of our alphabet. This net proved to be unique. In that net the Western world took all other cultures. No other culture originally took the step of separating the sound of words from their meanings and then of translating the sound into sight.

This fracturing of the integrity of the word split consciousness and culture into many fragments. It transferred the rich organic compound of immemorial speech into a thin abstract cross-section which could be examined at leisure and analysed.

The analysis of visually abstracted speech brought into existence very quickly the now traditional arts and sciences and their divisions. Today, simultaneity and inclusiveness of awareness is rapidly abolishing these divisions.

In the physical world we have the end of the age-old opposition between art and nature, as our technology reaches out to embrace light itself.

In the world of esthetics the poetic process has become the subject, plot and action of works of art. No more divisions of form and content, meaning and experience.

The new media—the new languages—which have increasingly supplemented writing and print, have begun to reassemble the multiple sensuousness of integral speech. Touch, taste, kinesthesia, sight and sound are all recreating that acoustic space which had been abolished by phonetic writing.

Under these conditions, prediction and evaluation are merely substitutes for observation. A basic feature of acoustic space is its inclusiveness. Visual space is exclusive. As our world recreates acoustic and oral culture by simply pushing on with devices of instantaneity and simultaneity, we need not fear the suppression of visual and written culture.

But the book will acquire, has already acquired, a major new role as tool of perception. It has long lost its monopoly as a channel of information. It can never lose its usefulness as a means of arresting thought and language for study. What the book was to the written manuscript, the LP disc is to music and radio.

Any change in any medium always causes modifications in all other media or languages within the same culture. Today in our simultaneous world such changes are felt as abrupt and drastic. They always were. But now we notice.

Let's now take a quick tour of the walls knocked over by media change.

Writing was the break-through from sound to sight. But with the end of the acoustic wall came chronology, tick-tock time, architecture. Writing, the enclosure of speech and sound space, split off song and dance and music from speech. It split off *harmonia* from *mimesis*.

Writing permitted the visual analysis of the dynamic logos that produced philology, logic, rhetoric, geometry, etc.

Modern physics and mathematics, like modern art before them, gradually abandoned visual for acoustic or non-Euclidean.

With writing on paper came the road. The road and paper meant organization at a distance: armies, empires, and the end of city walls.

But the manuscript was far from being the printed page. It was nearer to our photographic journalism. It had to be read slowly, aloud. The manuscript reader automatically found it easier to memorize all he read than refer again and again to this form. Until print, readers carried their lore at the tip of their tongues.

With print from moveable type (the first application of assembly-line method to a handicraft), came fast, silent reading.

Print knocked down the monastic walls of social and corporate study. The Bible: religion without walls.

But print isolated the scholar. It created the enterprising individual who, like Marlowe's Tamburlaine or Dr. Faustus, could over-run time and history and cultures and peoples.

Print evoked the walls of the classroom.

Print could channel so much information to the individual that had previously been in the mind and memory of the teacher alone, that it upset all existing educational procedures.

It upset the monopoly of Latin by making possible multi-lingual study.

It fostered the vernaculars and enlarged the walls between nations.

It speeded up language, thereby setting new walls between speech and song, and song and instrumentation.

Print led to spoken poetry and silently read poetry, thus changing the nature of verse entirely.

Printed music entirely changed the structures of musical forms.

In America print and book-culture became the dominant form from the beginning, setting walls between literature and art, and art and life, which were less obvious in Europe.

In America print was a technological matrix of all subsequent invention. Its assembly-lines finally reached expression in Detroit and the motor-car: the home without walls.

In America the press moulded public opinion and created a new base for politics.

The press was a means of mobilizing public opinion and made national road systems.

The press became in large measure a substitute for the book. But the press page is not the book page. The press creates new mental habits.

With telegraph only vernacular walls remain. All other cultural walls collapse under the impact of its instantaneous flash. With the wire-photo the vernacular walls are undermined.

The telegraph translates writing into sound. The electrification of writing was almost as big a step back towards the acoustic world as those steps since taken by telephone, radio, TV.

The telephone: speech without walls.

The phonograph: music hall without walls.

The photograph: museum without walls.

The movie and TV: classroom without walls.

Before print the community at large was the centre of education. Today, information-flow and educational impact outside the classroom is so far in excess of anything occurring inside the classroom that we must reconsider the educational process itself.

The classroom is now a place of detention, not attention. Attention is elsewhere.

It is now obvious that as all languages are mass media, so the new media are new languages. To unscramble our Babel we must teach these languages and their grammars on their own terms. This is something quite different from the educational use of audio-visual aids or of closed-circuit TV.

Marshall McLuhan

The Media Fit the Battle of Jericho
Marshall McLuhan - Unbound (16)

ISBN: 1-58423-051-7
Library of Congress Control Number 2005927213

Marshall McLuhan Unbound Project Editors
Eric McLuhan, W. Terrence Gordon

Published in United States in October 2005 by
Gingko Press, Inc.
5768 Paradise Drive, Suite J • Corte Madera, CA 94925
(415) 924-9615 • Fax (415) 924-9608
email: books@gingkopress.com
http://www.gingkopress.com

Design, packaging and production: Die Gestalten Verlag, Berlin
Layout and Typography: onlab, Berlin
Fonts: *Dolly* by Underware, *Bullet* by House Industries
Production: Martin Bretschneider, Vinzenz Geppert
Art direction: Robert Klanten

Made in Germany